THAILAND

WORLD ADVENTURES
BY STEFFI CAVELL-CLARKE

BookLife

BookLife
PUBLISHING

©2018
BookLife Publishing
King's Lynn
Norfolk PE30 4LS

All rights reserved.
Printed in Malaysia.

A catalogue record for this
book is available from the
British Library.

ISBN: 978-1-78637-513-1

Written by:
Steffi Cavell-Clarke

Edited by:
Robin Twiddy

Designed by:
Amy Li

THAILAND
WORLD ADVENTURES

CONTENTS

Words that look like **this** can be found in the glossary on page 24.

WHERE IS THAILAND?

THAILAND

MYANMAR

CAMBODIA

MALAYSIA

INDONESIA

Thailand is a country found in Southeast Asia. It is bordered by Myanmar, Laos, Cambodia, Malaysia and the Gulf of Thailand.

BANGKOK, THAILAND

The capital of Thailand is Bangkok.

The **population** of Thailand is over 68 million. Many people live in **rural** areas or large cities, such as Bangkok.

5

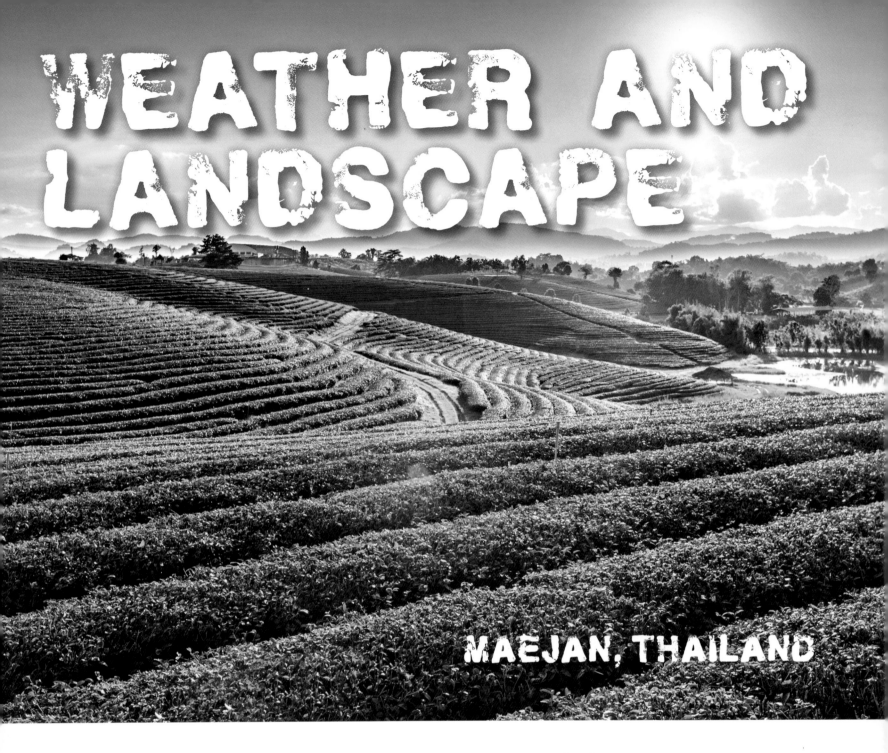

WEATHER AND LANDSCAPE

MAEJAN, THAILAND

Thailand has a **tropical climate** and three main seasons. They are the cool season, the hot season and the rainy season.

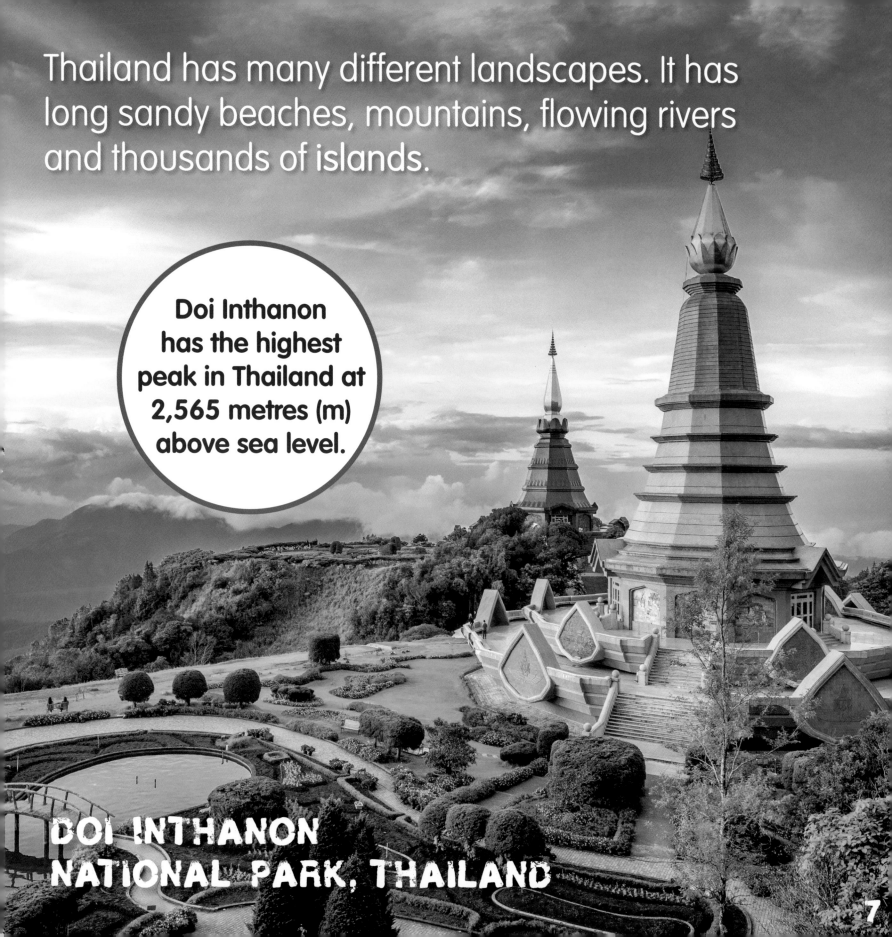

Thailand has many different landscapes. It has long sandy beaches, mountains, flowing rivers and thousands of islands.

Doi Inthanon has the highest peak in Thailand at 2,565 metres (m) above sea level.

DOI INTHANON
NATIONAL PARK, THAILAND

CLOTHING

Many people in Thailand wear **modern** clothing. There are many parts of Thailand where **traditional** clothing is still worn.

Traditional Thai clothing is usually very bright and colourful. Women often wear long dresses made from **embroidered** silk.

RELIGION

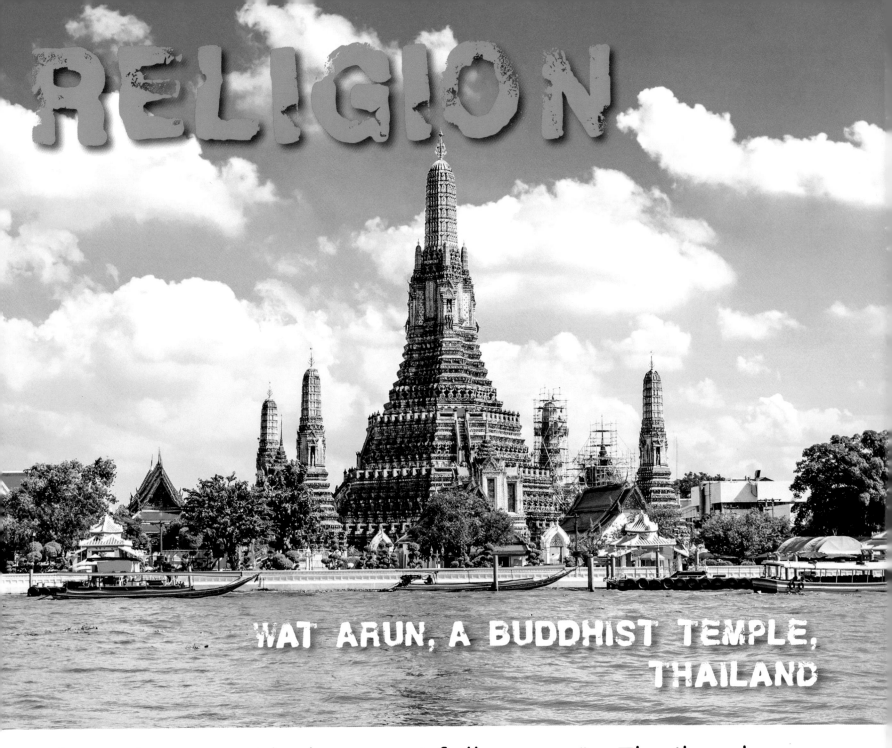

WAT ARUN, A BUDDHIST TEMPLE, THAILAND

The religion with the most followers in Thailand is Buddhism. There are over 30,000 temples in Thailand. This is where Buddhists worship.

Buddhist monks follow a strict set of rules that help them to live a simple and kind life. They often wear traditional orange robes.

These orange robes are called Kasaya.

FOOD

Thai food is famous around the world.
Popular dishes include curries, noodles and rice.

Thai food was traditionally eaten with hands while seated on mats on the floor. Today, most Thai people use chopsticks or a fork and spoon.

13

AT SCHOOL

Children in Thailand go to school from the age of 6 until they are 18. They study geography, maths, science and religion.

The main language spoken in Thailand is Thai.

Thai children also have to study a **foreign** language. They can study Chinese, French, Japanese, Russian, German or English.

AT HOME

Thai families can be very large and family members often live together. Many families live in small villages where they farm crops, such as rice.

Many people live in the big cities in Thailand. They often live and work in tall, modern buildings.

BANGKOK'S FINANCIAL DISTRICT

FAMILIES

Many children in Thailand live with their parents and brothers and sisters at home. They may also live with other family members, such as their grandparents.

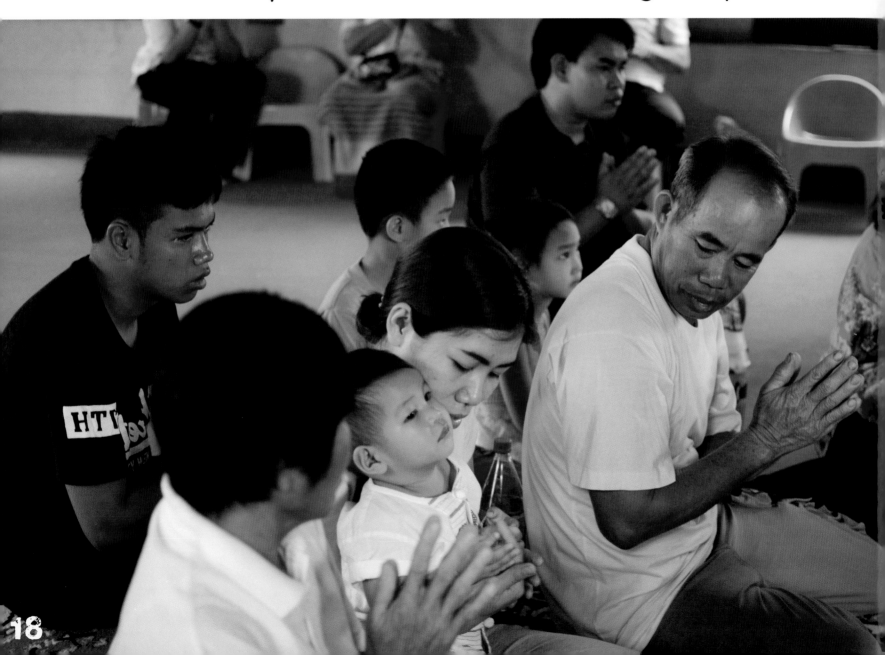

Thai families like to get together to celebrate special occasions such as religious festivals. They often celebrate by eating special food and singing songs.

SPORT

Muay Thai is a type of kickboxing that is very popular in Thailand. Two people fight each other by using their knees, shins, elbows and fists. It takes a lot of skill and practice.

Other popular sports in Thailand include volleyball, basketball and football. Many children learn how to play sports and swim at school.

FUN FACTS

Known as the Land of Smiles, Thailand welcomes millions of **tourists** every year. They go to see the tropical beaches, temples and the amazing wildlife.

Thai **folklore** is full of spiritual creatures such as ghosts and magical animals. There are hundreds of fairy tales that are still told to children today.

GLOSSARY

embroidered	patterns sewn into fabric
folklore	traditional beliefs or stories
foreign	another country or language
modern	something that has been recently designed
population	number of people living in a place
rural	relating to the countryside
tourists	people who visit another place for pleasure
traditional	ways of behaving that have been done for a long time
tropical climate	warm weather in a large area near to the equator

INDEX